To Jim's Youre Turn
APPOLOGIZE!
RDeutsch 02

RICHARD DEUTSCH SCULPTURE

Richard Deutsch: Sculpture was published on the occasion of the artist's exhibitions at the Gerald Peters Gallery, Santa Fe, New Mexico, 16 November–8 December 2001, and at the Museum of Art and History, Santa Cruz, California, 26 January–7 April 2002.

Published by the
Museum of Art and History
705 Front Street
Santa Cruz, California 95060

Library of Congress Number LC 2001-135487
ISBN 0-945952-03-1

Publication coordinated and written by Valerie Wolf Deutsch,
Davenport, California
Designed by Gordon Chun Design, Berkeley, California
Edited by Frances Bowles, Orinda, California
Printed in Korea through Overseas Printing Corporation, San Francisco, California

COVER: *Seven Stones,* 1999
Granite, 20 x 36 x 17 ft.
Collection of Anita and Ronald Wornick, St. Helena, California

Richard Deutsch Sculpture

Museum of Art and History
Santa Cruz, California

To Joseph Deutsch (1919–2001)

CONTENTS

Stacked Column, 1993

PREFACE

Richard Deutsch's family home and studio sit on a wooded ridge high above the California coast north of Santa Cruz. From the property, a distant view of the Pacific Ocean is framed in redwood trees. The proportions of this magisterial landscape have undoubtedly fed the heroic measure of his work.

While shaping a career that spans twenty-five years, Deutsch has pursued the skills and fostered the imaginative inquiry required to move from small-scale investigations in clay to monumental stone and bronze sculpture. As commissions and public artworks, these sculptures now reside across the United States.

His ease in understanding space and environment gives stature to Deutsch's work, his pieces an ingenious union of man-made and earth-born materials. These large-scale constructions require complex design and engineering abilities; the process is wrought with perplexities and challenges. Deutsch's temperament, a reassuring blend of patience and tenacity, has calmed many frayed nerves and led difficult projects to successful completion. The long-awaited exhibition of *Richard Deutsch: Sculpture* is now realized as a fully materialized display of the creative spirit.

Kathleen Moodie
Curator of Art, Museum of Art and History

ACKNOWLEDGMENTS

It is a rare occasion that the Museum of Art and History has the opportunity to publish such a comprehensive artist's catalogue as we are privileged to do with *Richard Deutsch: Sculpture.* The Museum of Art and History is fortunate to enjoy the support of a generous philanthropic community, which has provided the underwriting needed to present this exhibition and to document it with a significant publication. I also want to acknowledge and thank those individuals who contributed their time and talent to this effort. The insightful essay written by Bruce Guenther, Chief Curator at the Portland Art Museum, stems from his extensive involvement in the world of contemporary sculpture both as a curator and a historian. We are grateful for his contributions and perspectives to this book. In many of the photographs, the photographer Terrence McCarthy shares his keen eye with us. The graphic designer Gordon Chun, with his elegant sense of composition, has created a beautiful and classic book. Valerie Wolf Deutsch, whose firsthand knowledge of the artist's work and creative process, imbued all aspects of this project with a quiet dedication. Her efforts have resulted in a sincere and highly readable first survey of the sculptor's work.

I also wish to express my continuing appreciation of Curator of Art, Kathleen Moodie who was instrumental in organizing the exhibition. She worked closely with Richard Deutsch on the design of the installation and served as a resource for many of the professionals involved in this publication.

The artist joins us in thanking those who worked to realize both the sculptures and the installations, particularly Lud and Bud McCrary of Big Creek Lumber Company, Dorothy Goldeen Art Advisory, Gail Maxon-Edgerton, Director of Contemporary Art, Gerald Peters Gallery, and Robert Larson, Deutsch's studio assistant for the past eight years and an imaginative sculptor in his own right.

Last, I want to express my gratitude to the sculptor, Richard Deutsch, whom I have known as a member of the Santa Cruz art community for over twenty years. I respect his thoughtful professional manner and his clarity of purpose and applaud his focus and dedication.

Charles Hilger
Executive Director, Museum of Art and History

Richard Deutsch in Carrara, Italy, 1988

Richard Deutsch

by BRUCE GUENTHER

While at the American Academy in Rome in 1987, Richard Deutsch visited the ruins of Hadrian's Villa. There he experienced the equivalent of the Buddhist *satori*—a sudden enlightenment that changed the course and very nature of his work in the years that followed. Having been invited to spend a year at the American Academy in Rome by James Melchert, then its director and a fellow ceramic sculptor, Deutsch was encountering the riches of Italian art and the landscape of antiquity for the first time.

Richard Deutsch was born in Los Angeles, in 1953, into a cultured, middle-class Jewish family. He had traveled as a child, and between the ages of ten and twelve had lived in Israel. These early experiences eventually moved him to turn to making art. But he also grew up in Los Angeles within that phenomenon of change peculiar to the post–World War II years, when the incessant drumroll of the new surged across the landscape of California, transforming it from a bucolic agrarian state to the freeway-laced heart of the new American suburbia. Living in California's pervasive presentness, outside the deeper flow of history, Deutsch discovered that he was little prepared for the impact of his mature encounter with the complex physical layering of Italy's history and the resonance of its art.

Deutsch trained as a ceramist at the University of California, Santa Cruz, and began exhibiting his protosculptural forms on the West Coast in the late 1970s. Inspired by the traditions of Japanese Bizen and Shigaraki ceramics, and encouraged by Peter Voulkos to explore radical shifts of scale in the workshops he attended, Deutsch soon joined the ranks of ambitious young artists attempting to extend the material limits of clay toward a new sculptural presence. Deutsch made his own clay bodies and used wood-fired kilns, which enabled him to exploit clay's rich physicality as well as the unpredictable nature of the firing process to create a variety of forms that emphasize their material weight and surface in fresh ways. Evolving as a

Untitled ceramic construction, 1984

Untitled ceramic monolith, 1984

Untitled ceramic construction, 1984

Richard Deutsch in Carrara, Italy, 1987

sophisticated colorist in this period, Deutsch enjoyed great success in playing off his raw exploratory process, with its resulting awkwardness, against the highly designed forms and handsome color tonalities of his then-signature stelae.

Deutsch's clay work of the 1970s and early 1980s was often grounded in the form vocabulary of non-Western artifacts and primitive tools that combined strong silhouettes with an intense materiality. A series of clay monoliths produced in 1983 were to mark the last and largest of the strictly ceramic-based works in Deutsch's oeuvre. Ultimately finding himself frustrated by the physical limitations of clay, and seeking more permanent materials for his work, Deutsch began experimenting with combinations of various materials in a purely sculptural vocabulary. He had worked with a wide variety of clay processes, from wheel-thrown to coil and slab construction and even mold casting. Thus it was logical for him to look at materials that could be worked in similar ways and that offered possibilities for greater physical permanence and size. Using clay, concrete, and terrazzo (a cast material composed of marble or stone chips mixed into mortar, which can be polished when set), he began to assemble and cement together forms made from these different materials into works of a larger, more ambitiously public scale. It was during this period of experimentation with forms, materials, and surface finish that Deutsch accepted Melchert's invitation.

From the very beginning of his career, Richard Deutsch has focused on the materials of his work—what each medium is, and what can become of its limitations and possibilities—and the material completely informs his method and shapes the final artwork. Italy provided him with another layer

Pompeii and Hadrian's Villa, Italy, 1987

of possibility beyond the decorative aspects of obdurate matter; there he discovered a new reference point for the exploration of meaning and poetic association. Like generations of aesthetes before him, Deutsch found, in the layering of history revealed in the excavations and reconstruction of Pompeii and Hadrian's Villa, a sobering meditation on time and the fragility of self.

For Deutsch the Californian, Italy engendered a deeper sense of life's passages and revealed, as he said, "what age looks like." He realized, for perhaps the first time, that the physical erosion of time and the forces of change could be the source of sculpture and could suggest emotional meaning in his work. He reveled in the visceral surfaces of the ancient stones and the sculptural qualities of the architectural fragments in ruins that had survived or had been reassembled in another epoch. In earlier restoration efforts, the seemingly whimsical reconstruction of marble columns from fragments in which drums of different diameter and finish had been combined to reinvent an imagined whole, fascinated Deutsch. He studied the ways that an unfinished stone archway, jutting out into the air, could appear as sculpturally complete in its partiality as a Henry Moore bronze figure might in its abstraction. He found echoes of his continuing experiments with concrete and terrazzo in the manner by which some of the bits of architectural detail and the ruins had been reassembled with mortar, stone fragments, and cast concrete by anonymous workmen. Now removed from California's predictability, Deutsch experienced an epiphany that gave him "a source for a lifetime's work," and clarified the direction in which his art would move.

In his earlier use of primitive tools as a source of imagery for his ceramic work, Deutsch had already developed a fine sensitivity to the mysterious power of simple things. In the Italian interlude, he found an intensification of that core experience in a purely sculptural vocabulary. The manner in which the archeological assemblages resonated with an entirely different state of being from their original one gave Deutsch an important key to his next body of work.

In the *Restoration* series of the late 1980s, Deutsch introduced marble and various stones into his material vocabulary. These works reveal a new attitude of working that suggests equally the additive tradition of modern assemblage with its source in cubist collage and the more reductive, semi-abstract one that begins with Constantin Brancusi. A series of sculptures between five and eight feet high, the *Restoration* pieces incorporate cast terrazzo with carved and found-slab stone sections that were made, then broken, and then reassembled with the terrazzo into eloquent columnar works.

Initially, Deutsch found a ready source of inexpensive marble and granite slabs in the salvaged floors and toilet partitions from turn-of-the-century commercial buildings being torn down in San Francisco in the late 1980s and 1990s, though eventually he abandoned them for ever-larger blocks of stone. He pinned and glued the thin, salvaged slabs to build up larger volumes of stone, which could be carved, or to create striped light and dark patterns to play against a plain stone section in a finished work.

A series of multisegment stacked columns in a single material followed directly on the *Restoration* series in 1993. These abstract works, in their interlocking purity and almost hedonistically sensual materials, explore in a

Puzzle, from the *Restoration* series, 1987

more direct way the form of Brancusi's *Endless Column;* they suggest Deutsch's familiarity with similar work of older artists as diverse as Isamu Noguchi, Paul Feeley, and Carl Andre. Their interlocking forms—in stone, wood, or found metal such as ships' turnbuckles—gently suggest the softening segments of columns stacked on their sides, or vaguely bolsterlike shapes whose suggestion of softness belies the hard materials. Having previously built or constructed his forms, Deutsch became intrigued with objects such as the turnbuckle, which had a preexisting shape and dimension, and he began to search out materials with a past or a poetic possibility to reinvent or recontextualize as artwork.

12 At the end of the 1980s Deutsch, like many sculptors, found numerous opportunities for large-scale public and private commissions, and his artistic practice began to migrate away from the production of large bodies of studio work into the seductive realm of the public plaza. It is a now-familiar trajectory for many American artists of the post–World War II generations. The Art in Public Places movement offers the chance to work in collaboration with other artists, architects, and engineers on site-specific projects of an even larger architectural scale. Deutsch found this path to be of interest, and he has competed successfully for such commissions. He has presently realized some eight major public commissions in California in the 1990s and a series of significant private commissions for corporations and individuals in California, New Mexico, Tennessee, and Utah.

From 1989 through 1992, Deutsch was part of a seven-person design team charged with developing a plan to integrate art into a major commercial site in downtown Oakland, California, for what was then Bramalea Pacific Corporation. In the course of this process, Deutsch was to create two important sculptural works for the City Center development, along with a series of nine carved granite benches and a cascading water element. *Unity* (1991), a pair of granite sculptures sixteen feet high, marks either side of the main entrance to the tower building and comprises a multipart composition of horizontal and vertical stones. The stelae of *Unity* incorporate the full vocabulary of working stone—from drill holes for quarrying to rough, broken edges to mirrorlike, polished surfaces. They suggest both the rugged prehistoric raising of stones to mark a spiritual site and the post-apocryphal fragments of some demolished monumental past.

Turnbuckle, 1991

The second work, *Voyage* (1991–1992), occupies a wall thirteen feet high by thirty-two feet long in the building's West Plaza Garden. This work is constructed of massive, solid bronze ship propellers from the mothballed fleet of World War II Victory ships. *Voyage* is a relief of elegant rhythm created from the parsed sections of the enormous propellers. Though completely abstract, the work nonetheless suggests through the heroic associations of the material from which it is made the maritime history of the port of Oakland and the dynamic seagoing traffic of San Francisco Bay.

The Oakland Museum of California commissioned Deutsch to create a sculpture in 1994 to commemorate the museum's twenty-fifth anniversary and to celebrate its focus on the art, history, and ecology of California. Choosing as his theme the state's rich agricultural history, Deutsch incorporated granite and cast bronze elements into a complex and poetically evocative work titled *Harvest.* A massive, bladelike granite form that suggests an adze or a plow anchors the work to the earth. Building from it, Deutsch arranges and cantilevers a series of bronze forms cast from tractors and harvesting implements of the early twentieth century. Isolating their parts—a set of plow discs or a radiator cover—he emphasizes the abstract nature of the forms while still balancing the reference to their specific historic function. In Deutsch's complex composition, the bronze elements have been brought into an entirely different state of being from that of their source object. The sienna brown tonalities of the bronze patination was inspired by the rusted reality of the abandoned farm equipment that marks the landscape of California from the Klamath River Basin in the north to the last vestiges of the Irvine Ranch in southern California.

Whereas *Harvest* emphasizes its identity as a singular work of the artist's hand, Deutsch's commission for Stanford University in 1996 subsumes his unique vision into the larger ordering of the site and its furnishings. Located between two engineering buildings on the Palo Alto campus, *Axis* is a landscape of incident, a pure environment that seeks to reconcile the space between the disparate buildings of the Terman and Thornton Engineering Centers as a multiuse landscape. In Gibbons's Grove, Deutsch created a symbolic center for the site with a shallow basalt-paved dome, twenty-five feet in diameter, from which radiates a series of granite seating areas and a large stone table split through both its top and pedestal. Echoing the workings of the wheel—that monumental achievement of the earliest engineering technology—the artist's forms range from the massive table to the half-wheel-shaped benches. They also suggest elegant sculptural elements as furniture, in the tradition of the work of the late American sculptor Scott Burton. Although *Axis* lacks the artist's poetic voice as it is expressed in *Harvest,* it serves to intensify experience of the space and opens the mysterious power of simple, beautiful things to the casual participant.

Different in intention and effect are the works that Deutsch created in 1999 for the headquarters of the Applied Materials Corporation in Sunnyvale, California. Celebrating the importance of the silicon wafer to the advancement of high technology, *Etude* is a complex, highly symbolic work that incorporates carved and etched granite discs and cast bronze tools for measuring and calibrating. Leonardo da Vinci and his perpetual motion machine inspired the artist and led him to appropriate, for use on the stone discs, various motifs and drawings that suggest historic breakthroughs in humanity's efforts to understand the dynamics of the world in which we exist. With components located on either side of the driveway that is the main entry into the site, *Etude* provides an inspiring and inspired metaphor for the wonder of ideas and the business of high-technology research.

In 1999, Deutsch also completed one of the largest sculptures of his career, the magisterial *Seven Stones,* for a private residence in Napa Valley, California. Measuring a heroic twenty by thirty-six by seventeen feet, the granite work is inspired by the artist's memories of his travels in Italy and represents a new level of attainment in the formal language of his sculpture. The work is a synthesis of the technical prowess that Deutsch has achieved in working with stone, and of a formal vocabulary shaped by memory and the architecture of loss. Arcing across space, the massive stones seem almost weightless as they balance and intersect briefly in their tumble above the lawn. Like half-remembered fragments of Hadrian's Villa, or the echoes of his ceramic slab sculptures of 1983, *Seven Stones* gathers in the diverse experiences and sources of Richard Deutsch's life to project a dynamic new scale and tension for his sculpture. As one circles the work, the granite slabs, held together with stainless steel pins, exhibit a sophisticated rhythm of smooth and rough. Approaching the sculpture uphill from the entrance road, we see a series of ragged edges and rough-hewn surfaces absorbing light and evoking the ruggedness of the Sierra Nevada range. Circling back behind the work to stand on the terrace by the house to see the obverse is to experience for the first time its dazzling, mirror-polished planes defining and redefining the perceptual edges of the stone fragments and the surroundings. If it evokes for the artist the fragmented, soaring arches and crumbling porticos of Roman ruins, for me the work suggests the raw power of the Earth to throw up its mountains and shatter in a moment its peaceful plains. *Seven Stones* is a brilliant tour-de-force of the sculptor's art. It evinces a new quality of concentration and clarity for Deutsch that renders pictorial line and shape into physical fact.

The works in progress for the site-specific installation at the Museum of Art and History in Santa Cruz, California, promise to be some of the most beautiful of Deutsch's career and portend great things for the next phase of his production. With a handful of public commissions well in the works, Deutsch is moving back into the studio to struggle once more with the possibilities of the solitary object, to bring forward the majestic sobriety of stone, fusing mass and delicacy in a yet-to-be-seen paradigm of the spirit.

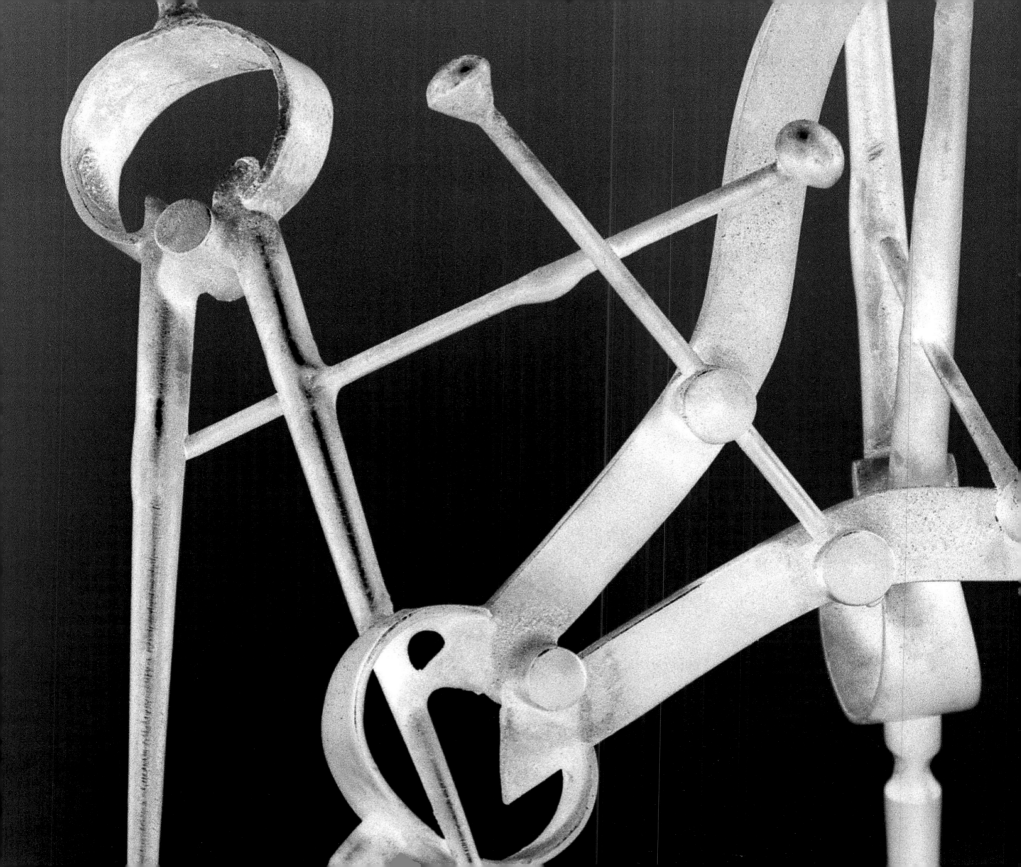

Sculpture 1985–2001

Black Slate, 1985

Untitled, 1985

Lean, 1987

Restoration, 1989

Stele, 1986

Untitled, 1989

FACING
Exhibition at the Sculpture
Court, Oakland Museum of
California, 1993

Left to right
Propeller, 1993
Stacked Column, 1993
Curves, 1993
Turnbuckle, 1991
Stacked Column, 1990

THIS PAGE
Turnbuckle, 1991

Shield, 1990

Passage, 1993

FACING
Stacked Column, 1996

THIS PAGE
Stacked Column, 1990

Stacked Column, 1999

Stone Table, 1999

Harvest Table, 1994

Curves, 1993

Red Hose, 1998

Dusk, 1997

Flock, 1997

Sown, 1997

Study for *Harvest*, 1994

Study for *Etude,* 1998

Relaxed Curves, 2001

Division, 2001

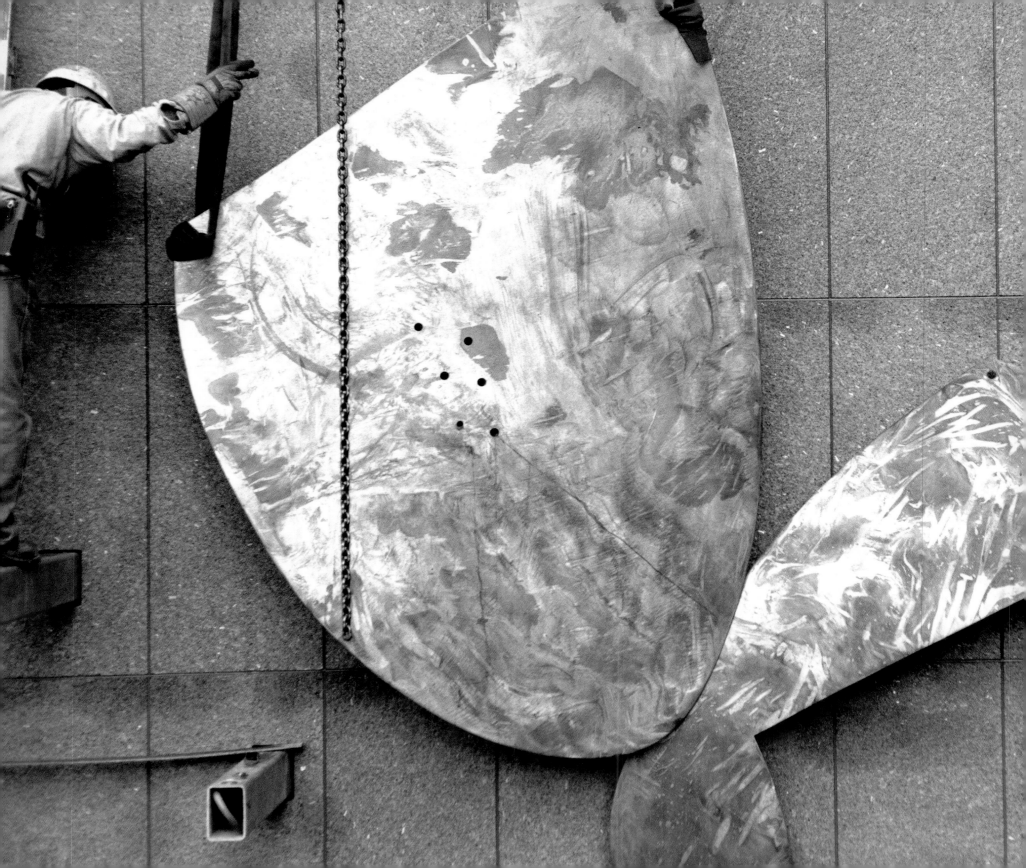

Projects 1989–1999

46   *Motion*, 1989
Wall relief, mixed media, 10 x 10 x 3 ft.
Port of Oakland, Oakland, California

In 1988, the Port of Oakland commissioned Richard Deutsch to create a
visually integrated lobby for its new
headquarters. Central to the project
is the wall relief *Motion,* a stone
sculpture *Lean,* stone seating,
and flooring. For *Motion,* the artist
searched the Port's waterfront
warehouses for parts of ships and
airplanes that had once transported
cargo to and from Oakland.

48

Voyage, 1991
Wall relief, World War II ship
propellers, bronze, 13 × 32 × 4 ft.
West Garden, 1111 Broadway Building
City Center, Oakland, California

Richard Deutsch participated as the
artist member of the design team
engaged to integrate art into the
building, plazas, and gardens of
1111 Broadway, a twenty-four-story
anchor building in Oakland's City
Center. Deutsch designed and
created sculpture environments for
the building's front and back plazas.

The focal sculpture in the West
Garden is the twenty-five-ton solid
bronze wall relief *Voyage,* made
from the propellers of World War II
Victory ships.

Voyage began in 1989 while Deutsch was searching through ship and airplane salvage for objects he could work into the sculpture *Motion* at the Port of Oakland. The shapes and complex curves of ship propellers intrigued him, and he began a decade-long investigation creating sculptures that incorporated these forms. When asked to join the City Center design team, he proposed an abstract wall relief of massive bronze propellers to reflect the importance of the waterfront to the city of Oakland.

Deutsch's proposal grew into an eighteen-month voyage involving not only the artist and his assistants, but also the developer Glenn Isaacson, Bramalea Pacific Corporation's entire project team, the building's anchor tenant, American President Companies, the City of Oakland, the United States Department of Transportation, a tug boat, a barge, a marine crane and crews, longshoremen, metallurgists, a lumber mill owner, a construction crane and crew, and the welders.

Deutsch learned of the Department of Transportation's mothballed fleets, primarily World War II Victory ships, in Suisan Bay, just north of Oakland. Stowed in the holds of some of those vessels were propellers that had been declared salvage. Through the auspices of the Redevelopment Agency and the City of Oakland, two massive bronze propellers were donated by the U.S. Merchant Marine to the city for this public art project.

For Deutsch, the project soon became a personal odyssey as well as an artistic one. Questions of aesthetics were coupled with the physical labor of cutting and shaping the monstrously large, hardened-bronze propellers and the necessity to meet deadlines tied to the timetables of the construction of the multistory skyscraper. Despite the difficulties, he was sustained and inspired by ideas that seemed to come from the propellers themselves.

Deutsch was captivated by the idea of transformation, the idea that these task-specific pieces of engineering—designed to live invisible lives under the sea, propelling people and cargo—could be completely transformed into a visible and tactile sculpture in which the overriding intent was a dialogue between shape and form.

54 *Voyage Plaza,* 1991
West Garden, 1111 Broadway Building
City Center, Oakland, California

The Voyage Plaza is a space for
people from City Center to convene.
Facing Deutsch's wall relief *Voyage*
on a grassy knoll are two asymmetri-
cal black granite sculpted benches
created from one solid stone. Directly
across the plaza from *Voyage* are
nine stone benches that the artist
sculpted in Carrara, Italy. These sit
in front of a water feature of river
rocks that he designed and created
in collaboration with the landscape
architect Paul Lettieri.

56

Unity, 1991
Monoliths, 16 ft. high, granite
East Garden, 1111 Broadway Building
City Center, Oakland, California

Unity consists of two granite compositions, each with five elements, that flank the front entry to the 1111 Broadway Building at Oakland's City Center. The intent was to create a visual unity to this urban plazascape, which stretches an entire city block, and to break the symmetry of a building designed on a symmetrical grid.

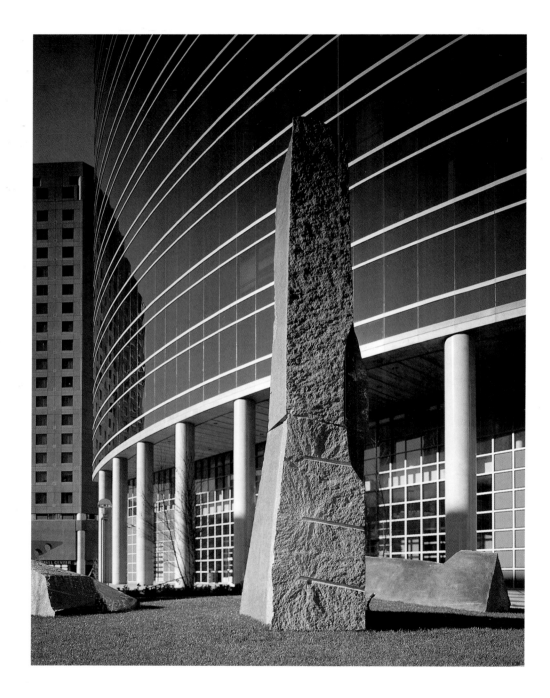

58

Solstice, 1991
Slate, 12 x 48 x 13 ft.
Private collection

The site for *Solstice* is an open
meadow of rolling hills from which,
year-round, both sunrise and sunset
may be observed unobscured. The
central element is a monolith, twenty
feet high, that casts a triangular
shadow onto the broad expanses of
these large slate stones. The artist
Tim Craighead (pictured left) assisted
Richard Deutsch with the installation.

60 *Harvest*, 1994
Granite, bronze, 10 x 15 x 15 ft.
The Oakland Museum of California

Harvest was commissioned by
patrons of the Oakland Museum
of California in celebration of the
museum's twenty-fifth anniversary.
Central to the composition is a
granite plow and bronze castings of
farm tools and machinery, including
a tractor hood, a combine, plow
discs, a tractor steering wheel, and
a shovel—all from the early 1900s.
In visually commemorating a stage
of California's agricultural history, the
sculpture ties together the museum's
three areas of focus—art, history,
and ecology.

While Deutsch was developing the concept for *Harvest,* Donn and Daisy Tognazzini invited him to work at their Diamond T Ranch in Los Olivos, California. There the artist photographed and cast molds of many of their historic farm implements and equipment. Ranchers and farmers, the Tognazzini family has worked this California land using many of these tools since the late 1800s.

Axis, 1996
Environment, Gibbons's Grove adjoining Terman and Thornton
Engineering Centers
Basalt dome, diameter 25 ft., granite table (32 in. x 13 x 11 ft.), granite seating areas
Stanford University, Stanford, California

Richard Deutsch was invited to design and create a multiuse environment that visually unifies the two engineering buildings on the site. This environment centers on a dome of basalt, which serves as a gathering place in Gibbons's Grove. Integrating the grove with the buildings are granite seating areas and a large stone table, all based on the workings of the wheel—a reference to the seminal achievement in the advancement of early engineering technology.

68

Etude, 1999
Sculptures and benches, granite and
bronze, 10 ft. high
Oakmead West, Sunnyvale, California

The sculpture and environment
Etude was commissioned for the
entrance to the campus of Applied
Materials Corporation. The sculpture
consists of two large granite discs,
referencing the silicon wafer, which
is at the root of the advancement of
modern high technology. The discs
are scribed, carved, and chiseled
with abstract drawings that are the
artist's interpretations of technologi-
cal breakthroughs. Integrated with
the discs are a large bronze compass,
calipers, dividers, and a micrometer,
depicting precise measurement and
calibration. Seven granite benches
provide an area for contemplation.

Etude

Seven Stones, 1999
Granite, 20 x 36 x 17 ft.
Collection of Anita and Ronald
Wornick, St. Helena, California

Seven Stones was inspired by the
artist's travels in Italy, of which the
countryside of the Napa Valley is
so often reminiscent. "The broken
columns, fragmented soaring arches,
and crumbled porticoes of Italian
ruins are very powerful to me as a
sculptor, not only for the objects
themselves, but as entire environments tangled with myth, circum-
stance, and imaginings. It is this
emotional and physical interaction
that I hope to capture with this
sculpture and environment."

Seven Stones

Seven Stones was created with support from Deutsch's dedicated team of sculptors and technical specialists, including his main assistant Robert Larson, the polisher Jorge Salguero, four riggers, a crane operator, a granite cutter, two core drillers, and the structural engineer John McLucus. Deutsch searched quarries in northern California and found the massive granite boulders just south of Yosemite National Park. There the arduous physical process of fabricating the sculpture began. A giant bulldozer moved the boulders so that they could be cut. Steel-braided wire saws were used to cut seven odd-shaped stone slabs, each weighing about ten tons. After the slabs were transported to the Napa Valley, they were split, cut, chiseled, drilled, notched, and polished. An eighty-ton, all-terrain crane was brought on site to suspend the gravity-bound slabs so that Deutsch and his crew could make the specific puzzle-like notched connections between the stones. The fifty tons of stones were then sprung together as an arch into their final positions. Once part of a mountain millions of years old, *Seven Stones* is now redefined and integrated in the gentle hills of Napa Valley.

AWARDS & EXHIBITIONS

AWARDS AND HONORS

1992   American Institute of Architects and Landscape Architects, East Bay, Orchid Award for *Voyage* sculpture at City Center, Oakland, California

1987   Visiting Sculptor, American Academy, Rome, Italy

1984   National Endowment for the Arts Visual Artist's Fellowship

SELECTED PUBLIC ART PROJECTS

2002   **Francis Newlands Johnston Park and William Sharon Farr Park, Chevy Chase Center, Washington, D.C.**: Art environment centered around water features for two urban plazas. Collaboration with William K. Hellmuth, AIA, senior principal, Suzette Goldsterin, AICP, Hellmuth, Obata+Kassabaum, P.C., and Don Hoover, principal, Oculus Landscape Architecture. Art adviser: Françoise Yohalem, Bethesda, Maryland. Commissioned by the Chevy Chase Land Company.

1999   **Oakmead West, Sunnyvale, California**: Sculpture and environment *Etude* for entry to high-technology campus. Art adviser: Cathy Baum and Associates, Atherton, California. Commissioned by CarrAmerica Realty Corporation, Washington, D.C.

1998   **California Science Center, Los Angeles, California**
Interactive water feature *Water Story* for the museum's central plaza. Part of a larger public art installation created by the artist Larry Kirkland. Commissioned by Larry Kirkland, Washington, D.C.

1996   **Stanford University, Terman & Thornton Schools of Engineering**
Sculptural environment *Axis.* Collaboration with the architects William Leddy and Marsha Maytum, AIA, principals, Tanner Leddy Maytum Stacy, San Francisco, and the landscape architect Peter Walker, Peter Walker and Partners, Berkeley, California. Commissioned by Stanford University.

1994   **Oakland Museum of California, Oakland, California**
Harvest. Commissioned for the museum's twenty-fifth anniversary by Friends of the Oakland Museum of California.

1991   **City Center, Oakland, California**
Member of design team engaged to integrate art into 1111 Broadway's plazas and gardens. *Unity,* two granite sculptures; *Voyage,* a solid bronze wall relief, nine granite benches, a granite footpath, and a water feature. Collaboration with architects from Gensler & Associates, San Francisco, and the landscape architect Paul Lettieri, of Guzzardo and Partners, San Francisco, California. Commissioned by Glenn Isaacson, Bramalea Pacific, Oakland, California.

1989 **Port of Oakland, Oakland, California**
Motion, wall relief; *Lean,* stone sculpture and stone seating. Collaboration on lobby design with Bill Donald, AIA, I.D.G. Architects, Oakland, California. Commissioned by Oakland Portside Associates, Oakland, California.

1988 **San Francisco Arts Commission, Art in Public Places Program**
Propeller, terrazzo artwork for Great Seawall Promenade. Commissioned by the City of San Francisco.

1987 **Washington State Arts Commission, Art in Public Places Program**
Stele, marble sculpture for Shelton Police Academy, Shelton, Washington. Purchased by the Washington State Arts Commission.

SOLO EXHIBITIONS

1977 Craft & Folk Art Museum, Los Angeles, California

1977 Long Beach Museum of Art, Long Beach, California

1979 Foster White Gallery, Seattle, Washington

1984 Foster White Gallery, Seattle, Washington

1984 B. Z. Wagman Gallery, St. Louis, Missouri

1989 Louise Allrich Gallery, San Francisco, California

1990 Louise Allrich Gallery, San Francisco, California

1993 Oakland Museum Sculpture Court, Oakland, California

1997 Foster White Gallery, Seattle, Washington

2001 Gerald Peters Gallery, Santa Fe, New Mexico

2002 Museum of Art and History, Santa Cruz, California

SELECTED GROUP EXHIBITIONS

1980 **American Porcelain: New Directions in an Ancient Art,** Renwick Gallery, Smithsonian Institution, Washington, D.C.

1982 **Pacific Currents,** San Jose Museum of Art, San Jose, California

1983 **Contemporary Expressions,** San Jose Institute of Contemporary Art, San Jose, California

1988 **Bay Area Sculpture: Metal, Stone, Wood,** Palo Alto Cultural Center, Palo Alto, California

1995 **Light Interpretations,** The Jewish Museum, San Francisco, California

1995 **Concept in Form: Artists' Sketchbooks & Maquettes,** Palo Alto Cultural Center, Palo Alto, California

1999 **The Art of Craft: Contemporary Works from the Saxe Collection,** M. H. de Young Memorial Museum, San Francisco, California

MUSEUM COLLECTIONS

Henry Art Gallery, University of Washington, Seattle, Washington

M. H. de Young Memorial Museum, San Francisco, California

Oakland Museum of California, Oakland, California

Renwick Gallery, Smithsonian Institution, Washington, D.C.

Stacked Column, 1993
Oak, 8 x 8 x 2 ft.
Collection of Linda Tirado and
Richard Strayer, Los Gatos,
California

Black Slate, 1985
Slate, 26 x 20 x 18 in.
Collection of Robert Farrar,
Los Angeles, California

Untitled, 1984
Ceramic, wood-fired, 39 x 21 x 17 in.
Collection of the artist

Untitled, 1985
Slate, marble, 32 x 16 x 14 in.
Private collection

Untitled, 1984
Ceramic, wood-fired, 66 x 27 x 12 in.
Collection of Gabriella and Glenn
Isaacson, Belvedere, California

Lean, 1987
Marble, 57 x 15 x 21 in.
Collection of the artist

Untitled, 1984
Ceramic, wood-fired, 28 x 24 x 19 in.
Collection of the artist

Restoration, 1989
Marble, terrazzo, 68 x 23 x 8 in.
Collection of Shari and Garen Staglin,
Rutherford, California

Puzzle, from the *Restoration* series, 1987
Marble, 96 x 14 x 5 in.
Private collection

Stele, 1986
Marble, terrazzo, 85 x 28 x 13 in.
Private collection

Untitled, 1989
Marble, 84 x 22 x 16 in.
Private collection

Stacked Column, 1990
Granite, 62 x 23 x 21 in.
Collection of the artist

Turnbuckle, 1991
Cast iron, 60 x 24 x 24 in.
Collection of the artist

Stacked Column, 1999
Basalt boulders, 15 ft. high
Collection of Sandie Tillotson, Sandy, Utah

Shield, 1990
Marble, granite, 65 x 28 x 18 in.
Collection of Gabriella and Glenn Isaacson,
Belvedere, California

Stone Table, 1999
Granite, 31 in. high x 20 x 5 ft.
Collection of Sandie Tillotson, Sandy, Utah

Passage, 1993
Marble, granite, terrazzo, 8 x 8 x 2 ft.
Collection of Dorothy and George Saxe,
Menlo Park, California

Harvest Table, 1994
Granite, 31 in. high x 18 x 4½ ft.
Collection of Shari and Garen Staglin,
Rutherford, California

Stacked Column, 1996
Granite, 9 x 4 x 4 ft.
Private collection

Curves, 1993
Terrazzo, 5 x 17 x 17 ft.
Private collection

Red Hose, 1998
Mixed media 42 x 36 x 12 in.
Collection of the artist

Dusk, 1997
Bronze, 39 x 42 x 12 in.
Collection of the artist

Flock, 1997
Bronze, 30 x 92 x 10 in.
Private collection

Sown, 1997
Bronze, 45 x 80 x 20 in.
Collection of the artist

Study for *Harvest,* 1994
Bronze, 7 x 6 x 4 in.
Collection of the artist

Study for *Etude,* 1998
Bronze, 5 x 5 x 4 in.
Collection of the artist

Relaxed Curves, 2001
Granite, 4 ft. 6 in. x 8 x 6 ft.
Courtesy of Gerald Peters Gallery,
Santa Fe, New Mexico

Division, 2001
Terrazzo, 6 ft. 8 in. x 6 ft. 2 in. x 8 in.
Courtesy of Gerald Peters Gallery,
Santa Fe, New Mexico

Motion, 1989
Wall relief, mixed media, 10 x 10 x 3 ft.
Collection of the Port of Oakland,
Oakland, California

Voyage, 1991
Wall relief, ship propellers, bronze, 13 x 32 x 4 ft.
Installation at 1111 Broadway, City Center,
Oakland, California
Collection of the Shorenstein Company,
San Francisco, California

Voyage Plaza, 1991
Nine granite benches, granite footpath, river-rock
water feature
Installation at 1111 Broadway, City Center,
Oakland, California
Collection of the Shorenstein Company,
San Francisco, California

Unity, 1991
Monoliths, each with five elements, granite;
16 ft. high
Installation at 1111 Broadway, City Center,
Oakland, California
Collection of the Shorenstein Company,
San Francisco, California

Solstice, 1991
Slate, 12 x 48 x 13 ft.
Private collection

Harvest, 1994
Granite, bronze, 10 x 15 x 15 ft.
Collection of the Oakland Museum of California

Axis, 1996
Basalt dome (diameter 25 ft.), granite table (32 in. x
13 x 11 ft.), granite seating areas
Installation at Gibbons's Grove, Stanford University
Collection of Stanford University

Etude, 1999
Sculptures, granite, bronze, 10 ft. high
Benches, granite
Installation at Oakmead West, Sunnyvale, California
Commissioned by CarrAmerica Realty Corporation,
Washington, D.C.

Seven Stones, 1999
Granite, 20 x 36 x 17 ft.
Collection of Anita and Ronald Wornick,
St. Helena, California

BIBLIOGRAPHY

Blasier, Paula. *Voyage: From Ship's Propeller to Sculpture.* Oakland, Calif.: Bramalea Pacific, 1991. Includes a photo essay by Terrence McCarthy.

Broadrup, Elizabeth. "Motion: Wall Relief at Port of Oakland." *Sculpture Magazine* (November/December 1990).

Burgard, Timothy Anglin. *The Art of Craft: Contemporary Works from the Saxe Collection,* exh. cat. San Francisco: The Fine Arts Museums of San Francisco; Boston: Bulfinch Press/Little, Brown, 1999.

Clifton, Leann. "An Oakland Odyssey." *Artweek* (29 January 1992).

Fuhrman, Janice. "A Napa Family Vineyard." *California Homes Magazine* (October 2000). Article about the Staglin Family Vineyard art collection.

"Harvest." *Sculpture Magazine* (July/August 1995). Article on Deutsch's commission for the Oakland Museum of California.

Mayer, Barbara. "Dream House for a Dream Collection." *Art & Antiques* (April 2000). Article about the Wornick family art collection.

Misrach, Myriam Weisang. "Ideas Beneath the Surface: Richard Deutsch." *The Museum of California* (magazine of the Oakland Museum of California) (winter 1993).

Narain, R. Kamna. "Public Art." *The Business Journal* (October 1998). Article describing Deutsch's project for Oakmead West in Sunnyvale, California.

Suter, P. "Integrating Art into Development." *Urban Land Magazine* (September 1991).

All photographs by Terrence McCarthy except as noted.
Tim Craighead, 9 (studio); Richard Deutsch, 10 (bottom and second from bottom), 58, 59, 62 (top left and right), 63, 79 (right, top to bottom); Tony Grant, 11, 12, 16, 17, 18, 19, 20, 21, 22, 24, 27, 47; Joel Leivick, 8; Robert Larson, 79 (left); Mark Primack, 10 (top, left to right); Rick Surlow, 9 (artwork).